The New Reform Agenda

by

Howard A. Snyder

First Fruits Press
Wilmore, Kentucky
c2012

asburyseminary.edu
800.2ASBURY
204 North Lexington Avenue
Wilmore, Kentucky 40390

First Fruits
THE ACADEMIC OPEN PRESS OF ASBURY SEMINARY

ISBN:9780914368939
ISSN 1090-5642

The Asbury Journal
Volume 61, 2006
Number 1 (Spring), Number 2 (Fall)

Digital version at http://place.asburyseminary.edu/asburyjournal/

First Fruits Press
B.L. Fisher Library
Asbury Theological Seminary
204 N. Lexington Ave.
Wilmore, KY 40390
http://place.asburyseminary.edu/firstfruits

Morrison, H. C. (Henry Clay), 1857-1942.
    Sermons for the times / by H.C. Morrison.
    Wilmore, Ky. : First Fruits Press, c2012.
    138 p. ; 21 cm.
    Reprint. Previously published: Previously published: Louisville, Ky. :
Pentecostal Publishing Company, c1921.
    ISBN: 9780984738649 (pbk.)
    1. Sermons, American. 2. Methodist Church—Sermons.. I. Title.
BX833 .M6 S4 2012

Cover design by Haley Hill

asburyseminary.edu
800.2ASBURY
204 North Lexington Avenue
Wilmore, Kentucky 40390

First Fruits
THE ACADEMIC OPEN PRESS OF ASBURY SEMINARY

The New Reform Agenda

Howard A. Snyder

2011 Howard A. Snyder

The United States is in critical need of massive reform. The same could be said of many other nations, but my focus here is the U.S.

From one angle, reform is always needed, and typically reform surges run in generational cycles. But today is especially critical. For a host of reasons—among them the increasing complexity of society and of international relations—the spectrum of critical issues that must be addressed *immediately* is huge, unprecedented. They range from matters of physical infrastructure to large-scale issues of the mind, heart, and spirit.

I will give a quick inventory and overview in a moment.

Things are stirring in U.S. society today—deep things now surfacing in "Occupy Wall Street" and other movements.

But first and crucially, *we must think ecologically.* Every pressing need is linked to all the others. There is an ecology to our problems. Beginning to solve one helps solve others; failure to address one aggravates others. Yet obviously some are especially critical.

First, an inventory. When I conceived this article, I quickly came up with a random list of some thirty items, ranging from agriculture to prisons to United Nations reform (certainly a U.S. concern). Each of these in turn is complex; many are interconnected; all cry out for attention; bright red flags.

Here is my alphabeticized, unprioritized, and overlapping list—all areas needing major reform: Aging and nursing care, agriculture (including food and diet), the arts (including music and literature), business, childcare, climate change, Congress, crime, education, energy (including buildings and building codes), entertainment, environmental policy, government regulation, healthcare, immigration, infrastructure, international finance, international relations, the judiciary and law, labor, marriage (including family life and sexuality issues), medicine, the military, mining, prisons, public safety, religious practice and tolerance, science and technology, substance abuse, transportation (rail, highway, air, public transportation generally), the United Nations.

U.S. society is massively dysfunctional in many of these areas, and many others certainly need improvement. Not all are public policy issues, of course, but many are. All have spiritual and social dimensions. Lumped altogether and left unaddressed, they could spell disaster for the United States and the world.

Is there any hope? Yes! If you know anything about reform movements in U.S. history and more broadly in culture, and if you believe God is somehow at work in history, the answer has to be yes. Shorter-term or longer-term.

Given the current state of the U.S. and the world, it *must* be shorter-term.

Seven Top Priorities

What are the top priorities? With such a fluttering flock of front-row issues, it may seem hard to decide. But here is a test: If we think ecologically, which issues pop to the top? Which seven issues (for instance) if addressed head-on would make the biggest difference and have the greatest impact on the others? Which, if addressed, would most strategically interact together ecologically, with the maximum number of positive feedback loops and minimal negative feedbacks?

Due to the so-called "law of unintended consequences" and other factors, we can't know fully. However I believe these *seven emerge as top priorities* when examined separately and in connection with the others: climate change, education, infrastructure, agriculture and food, energy policy, transportation, and international finance. Key specific reforms in these areas would, quite literally, change the world.

1. Climate Change

This is the most pressing for two reasons: First, because it affects everything, since it literally concerns the environment in which everything else occurs. Second, because it is time-critical. The longer the delay in addressing it, the more challenging the solutions become and the longer it will take to reverse dangerous climate trends.

The two big priorities here are the creation of a global price for carbon and the switch to "green" (renewable) energy and technology globally and across the board. Some countries in Europe (and the Euro-Zone generally) are way ahead of the U.S. and China in these areas, and some small steps are being taken here and there. But nowhere near enough, nor with sufficient urgency.

These reforms in turn would help bring about other much-needed changes: Major reductions in deforestation, species depletion, coal mining by mountain-top destruction, air and water pollution, and other forms of environmental rape.

Benefits: The major benefit will be a healthier climate for everyone, especially the poor—though things are now so bad that the climate will get more erratic and dangerous for decades, until the situation perhaps gradually improves. But there are many auxiliary benefits relating to greater sensitivity toward the environment, all earth's peoples, and a more ecological understanding of economics. (See Daley & Farley, *Ecological Economics*; Lappé, *EcoMind*.)

Danger: If climate change is not addressed quickly, comprehensively, and intelligently, the biggest danger is not the extensive damage from erratic weather. It is that the world's big economies will try to adjust to it by technological and business fixes, making things much worse and potentially more lethal, with possible wars over water and other declining resources.

2. Education

The United States is falling way behind other advanced nations in primary and secondary education. A poorly education citizenry clearly hampers everything else. Globally, U.S. students are trailing in math and science. Many students can't even find their own town or city on a map without accessing the Internet. Dropout rates are often horrendous.

The current economic downturn is made much worse by this dismal educational situation. To a large degree high unemployment is as much a *skills* crisis as it is a *jobs* crisis. People can't find work because they don't have the necessary education and training. Tens of thousands of jobs go begging for lack of qualified applicants.

So education reform is a big deal. Like climate, it affects virtually everything else. The matter is complex because failing schools are often in part a function of failing families—something the educational system can't solve.

Many good reform measures are now on the table, from reforming "No Child Left Behind" to extending the school day and year. Students must be taught essential *content* in math, science, history, art, literature, and other areas, and they must be taught *reflective critical thinking*—something that good teaching in art, literature, and science can provide.

Comprehensive educational reform would strengthen public schooling; encourage the smart use of charter schools and other innovations; and find ways to provide more integration and cross-referencing between public schooling and home-schooling.

Benefits. Improved education will give a big boost to the economy and to U.S. creative competitiveness globally. More importantly, it will raise the level of citizenship and civic involvement, thus improving the political process and "securing the general welfare." Better informed citizens will mean more public support for dealing with environmental and other issues and broader backing for the arts. It will have a positive impact on other issues discussed here.

Danger: If education reform is not effectively addressed, the fabric of society will continue to unravel. The gap between rich and poor will gape wider.

Either way, the U.S. will pay: Either smart investments in education—or if not, increasing billions for welfare, crime-fighting, prisons, and multiple social ills. Education in itself doesn't solve social ills, but a poorly-educated citizenry is fatally handicapped in developing a responsible and responsive society.

3. Infrastructure

"Infrastructure" covers a lot, but here I speak mainly of physical things—bridges, streets and highways, utilities (electricity, water, sewage, communications), railroads, airports, oil and gas mains, dams and dikes, flood control—all the essential structures on which daily life depends, and which we think of only when disaster strikes. All of these are heavily funded, regulated, or subsidized by government (local, state, federal). So they are matters of civic interest and responsibility. Since they necessarily involves taxation, these areas are easily neglected and frequently under-funded, often falling victim to politics.

Three things must happen. At the federal level, a major infrastructure rebuilding program should be launched, perhaps using President Obama's proposal of an "infrastructure bank." Second, states, municipalities, and regional authorities must make infrastructure a much higher priority.

Third, tax and other government policies should be revised in order to (1) keep economic growth more or less in sync with infrastructure development, (2) move infrastructure in a much more ecologically responsible direction, and (3) maintain a constructive cooperative partnership between business, government, universities, and private philanthropy in infrastructure development so that systems are rational, functional, and reasonably well coordinated. Infrastructure projects and reforms often work best when there is an intelligent partnership (or joint venture) between government and industry. (History here is mixed; outstanding successes, and dismal failures due either to poor design or corruption. So intelligence and wisdom, not inaction, are needed.)

As noted below, *transportation policies and priorities* also need reworking as part of the infrastructure question.

Benefits: Infrastructure improvements benefit everyone. They contribute to the general welfare, making life easier and less aggravating. They facilitate business success, and thus economic vitality. Consider the difference, for instance, between having safe bridges, efficient power lines and pipelines, and safe drinking water, on the one hand, and having power outages, broken gas mains, collapsing bridges, and polluted or no water on the other.

We take such utilities for granted, but they are not automatic or permanent. Like one's own house, constant maintenance and attention are required. Wise reforms however would produce a much more civil society (removing a lot of the friction and grit in the machine, as it were), thus facilitating reforms and improvements in other areas, as well.

Danger: If infrastructure is not attended to regularly and wisely, the dereliction will be a drag on the whole society—a damper on the economy and a contributor to social malaise and unrest. Infrastructure breakdown can lead to social breakdown. Especially when it combines with deterioration in other areas discussed here, such as climate change and education.

4. Agriculture and Food

The United States is in the middle of a toxic food crisis which is also an agriculture and health crisis—and hardly knows it.

Every person should be able to answer four basic food questions: What is it? Where did it come from? How did it get here? Is it good for me? But most Americans today, and millions of others in the increasingly globalized industrial food market, simply can't answer these most basic questions. If people look at the list of ingredients, they are quickly mystified by unknown chemical compounds and unfamiliar technical terms. We simply have no idea how much of our food comes from factory farms, laboratories, and fossil fuels, rather than from healthy farms that nurture and preserve the earth. Often we simply do not know what we are eating. (See for example *The Omnivore's Dilemma: A Natural History of Four Meals*, by Michael Pollan, 2006.)

The problems with agriculture and food, especially in the U.S., are many and complex. The basic problem is that we have an unhealthy agricultural system: Too much reliance on chemicals, government subsidies, intensive farming, monoculture, and unsustainable consumption of water; too little organic farming, variety, sustainable land use, and ecological sensitivity. Relatedly, high-intensity industrialized farming nationally and globally means that fruits and vegetables are often harvested before they are fully ripe, dowsed in coloring or preservatives to make them look better than they are, and shipped long distances at the cost of fossil-fuel consumption and pollution. The result is food that is literally *unnatural* and often nearly tasteless. Fortunately, some counter-trends are now at work—for instance, more locally-grown food, farm markets, and urban agriculture.

The reform agenda here: A shift in national and international agriculture policies away from supporting large-scale industrial food and flavor production and toward facilitating organic and local food, much improved public information, and much greater attention to environmental sustainability.

<u>Benefits</u>: These reforms would, for starters, produce these benefits: 1) a physically and socially healthier society, 2) a more vibrant and sustainable economy, and 3) healthier land (including woodlands, streams, rivers, and parks)—and, over decades, a more pleasant and life-giving climate.

It will be a great day in America when people discover what real food actually tastes like rather than dining on factory-made chemicals ("natural and artificial flavors") that now provide the taste in most processed food. When people discover that "natural flavors" are not natural at all, but are laboratory-produced compounds made from organic substances that have been "enhanced" by salts and sugars so that they become semi-addictive, they may awaken to the joy of healthy, flavorful eating. (The only difference between "natural" and "artificial" flavors is the original source of the chemicals, whether organic or inorganic.)

<u>Danger</u>: If agriculture and food production are not reformed, the result is clear: More obesity, increased incidence of disease, declining national health in comparison to the rest of the world. Healthcare costs will soar much more than they need to. Perhaps more importantly, without reform the food and agriculture system will increase global warming, to the detriment of people everywhere—especially the poor.

5. Energy Policy

This also is huge, since all life is energy and all life depends on energy, especially from the sun. How energy is produced, processed, utilized, and wasted affects everything else. It is also closely linked with climate change.

A key fact that should stick in everyone's head: Consuming energy always produces waste in addition to useful work. We know this from the laws of physics (thermodynamics) and from the life sciences. No form of energy is 100% efficient or 100% renewable. Thus no "perpetual motion machine." The issue is: Which forms of energy production, consumption, and recovery are most efficient, and thus most renewable and sustainable?

We know that most of the energy produced by an incandescent light bulb is lost as heat. Same with the internal combustion engine, though here other toxic pollutants also result. In fact, in energy production worldwide, 40% or more is wasted. So conservation is the biggest source of new energy.

Energy policy in the U.S. is a mess, all tied up with the huge fossil-fuel industry and the sprawling transportation industry (especially automobiles, SUVs, trucks, and airplanes).

The major problem here is that the mushrooming burning of fossil fuels since industrialized coal mining began in the 1700s has brought normal climate-change cycles to the tipping point, endangering the whole planet.

Biofuels such as Ethanol are not the answer. Biofuel production wastes energy and often diverts food products into fuel manufacture, driving up food prices, which especially harms the poor.

The obvious big reforms here are two: 1) switching from fossil fuels to more sustainable sources (solar, lunar [harnessing tides], wind, and thermal, especially), and 2) vastly increasing the energy efficiency of our entire infrastructure, from building design to power systems to transportation. This second reform is much less controversial and more easily achieved, so should be given high priority. But both are necessary, and long-term the shift to eco-friendly energy is the more crucial.

Sustainable energy is necessary all across the board, in all areas of human life, from residences to transport to public utilities. This must happen first of all for environmental reasons. But benefits accrue in many other areas: economic life, ease of living, and even aesthetics.

The necessary technology is already available (and in use here and there) to make sustainable (mostly renewable) energy available to meet the greater part or the nation's and the world's needs. Skeptics have said for years that "green" energy could never meet more than ten percent of the nation's energy needs, but in many places this is being proven wrong.

More and more auto companies are producing hybrid or all-electric vehicles; surely both the technology and the acceptance of these will increase (though hybrid and electric vehicles also pollute). In a number of places businesses, large retail stores, and cities are installing recharging stations. Solar and wind applications are increasing, especially in advanced countries outside the U.S. Renewable energy is one of the bright spots in an otherwise stagnant economy.

We are at the leading edge of an energy revolution. The problem is that it is coming much too slowly and in too piecemeal a fashion, with major resistance from some folks in government and industry. Intelligent nationwide policies to speed this revolution, including a major push to recycle and conserve energy, are urgently needed.

Benefits: Like the other reforms, and combined with them, energy reforms would produce a more livable environment and a more flourishing and pleasant society. *Sustainability* is actually a very positive, sound, and aesthetically pleasing concept and reality. We know this in our own lives, physical health, and finances, and the same is true globally. Sustainability is a more ecologically sound value than is *growth*. Growth is good only to the degree that it operates within a dynamic sustainable system.

The main benefit of fundamental energy reform is not what will happen, but rather what will be avoided. Therefore—

Danger: If energy policy is not deeply reformed climate change will accelerate, bringing more and more "weird weather" to North America and the whole globe. Sea levels will rise; more and more species will become extinct; normal patterns of transportation, agriculture, and social life will be disrupted. This will have huge political and economic, and thus very likely military, consequences. Increasingly there will be a polarizing tension between the haves and the have-nots, both in the U.S. and globally. In multiple ways, quality of life will deteriorate for everyone. Famines of unprecedented scale will likely loom.

These consequences are mostly avoidable if major reforms occur quickly. Not totally avoidable, because the long-term effects of unwise energy policy will continue for decades before significant improvement happens.

6. Transportation

Most of the issues discussed so far, especially energy, involve transportation. We must say more about that specifically.

My concern here is mostly with large transportation systems, whether commercial, government-run (federal, state, regional, local), or a combination of the two: Railways, highways, airlines, and urban mass-transit systems.

These are all huge energy users. Significant progress is being made in switching to much more energy-efficient electric or hybrid locomotives, and the efficiency of airliners has improved substantially over the past ten years. But much more needs to be done.

Our passenger railway system is inefficient and obsolete. It is almost totally inadequate in terms of the need and the potential. Much of it runs on railways built a century or more ago. This sad picture is painfully obvious when compared with Europe, China, Japan, or South Korea. The U.S. sorely needs a high-speed, environmentally friendly, nationwide rail system. It can be built, and in some other countries *is* being built. The technology is available and well known. Economic resources are sufficient, if the political will could be mustered.

We have known for more than a century that steel wheels moving on steel rails is generally the most efficient mode of mass transit and transport. The benefits of a "green" nationwide rapid rail system are many. Two big ones: (1) reduced auto traffic and congestion, and (2) greater efficiency in air travel. If airport hubs were directly linked by rapid-rail transport, many fewer regional flights would be necessary. One could travel for instance from Detroit to Chicago, or Cincinnati to Cleveland, more quickly and conveniently by rail than by air, eliminating much of the time it takes to get to an airport, go through security, walk to the gate, wait for the departure time, go through a long and cramped boarding process—then repeat the same on arrival. Much easier to make the trip on an efficient train, or to travel by rapid rail to a major airport and there transfer quite efficiently to an international or transcontinental flight. Today this is possible at only a few U.S. airports.

Seasoned travelers know that an hour or two on a modern train is much more comfortable, less confining, more time efficient, and less hassle than an hour's plane ride. Also, there is usually less danger and anxiety in traveling along the surface of the earth than in soaring high above it.

Similar dynamics apply to urban mass transit. Simply adopting an electric urban rail system similar to that found in Swiss cities, for instance, would make U.S. cities much more livable. It would enhance urban life generally, helping to promote arts and culture because of the added convenience. If done in an environmentally sound way, it would make both urban life and the global ecosystem more sustainable.

With this should come, as another reform, a reversal of the trend to keep expanding urban freeway systems. The national Interstate highway system has served its purpose and should be phased back as rapid-rail systems expand. Ninety percent or so of the cargo that travels by large trucks on highways should be moved by rail (primarily) and by air and rivers. (The considerable expansion of "piggyback" tractor trailers on railroad cars is a step in the right direction.)

Such phasing back is especially needed in cities. Over the past twenty years we have witnessed the stark "uglification" of the urban Interstate system. Today in Indianapolis, for instance, ugly concrete walls are going up along big sections of I-465, which rings the city. While this helps protect residential areas from noise and pollution, it creates long concrete corridors blocking off motorists' views—ugly gray canals and caverns that are virtually identical nationwide. This is a disgrace and the opposite of what was originally intended. It has negative social effects, blocking off local neighborhoods from each other, extending the gap between rich and poor, and in general making urban life less enjoyable and esthetic.

These reforms should be accompanied by urban planning that makes other low-impact forms of transportation, such as walking and bicycling, convenient and practical—as many cities are in fact now doing. Relatedly, there should be a gradual switchover from four-way stops on major streets to traffic roundabouts (as in England). Carmel, Indiana, has begun such a switchover and is already seeing fewer accidents and traffic deaths and less vehicular pollution.

If we think *ecologically,* we can see how such reforms in transportation reinforce reforms in other areas.

Benefits: As already noted, transportation reforms would make daily life more convenient, pleasant, and economical. More important from a systemic perspective, they would contribute to a more viable and vibrant global economy and a more sustainable environment.

Danger: Without these reforms, the trend lines toward increasing dysfunction, inconvenience, aggravation, and ecological destruction will rise sharply. The U.S. needs to reverse destructive cycles in transportation and increase "virtuous cycles" of convenience and sustainability.

7. International Finance

This is a biggie, but it is invisible to maybe ninety percent of the population. It hugely affects politics and business, and is largely unregulated.

Existing global systems provide limited safeguards and standards in some areas of economics and international relations, but not in global finance. International finance is a world unto itself. It dwarfs in size the economies of most nations and is aimed at one thing: Profit from financial transactions. The system has rightly been called "making money from making money."

Today the global economy (and with it much of our wellbeing) is held hostage to a "global casino in which $1.3 trillion worth of derivatives, credit default swaps and other financial instruments slosh around every day without a hint of concern or regard for the millions of lives that such speculation can destroy," as Kalle Lasn and Micah White put it in a November 18, 2011, article in *The Washington Post*.

The ongoing financial crisis in Europe is the current best example. World financial markets often bet *against* economic recovery and financial stability—which acts like a self-fulfilling prophecy. The more financial markets think a country or bank or company will fail, the more they raise the price of money, thus making default all the more likely. In this sense truly "It is all about confidence," as several economists have said.

These multi-trillion-dollar speculations in currency and credit are the global equivalent of neighborhood loan sharks and ought to be illegal.

The major reform needed here: Creation of a Global Reserve System similar to the U.S. Federal Reserve ("The Fed"). The U.S. Federal Reserve System was created in 1913 after a series of financial panics. It helps keep the U.S. economy reasonably stable. But now the global financial system is much larger than any country and operates like a series of sovereign monetary states. It cannot be reined in without an effective Global Reserve System created cooperatively by the nations of the world.

The United States, in collaboration with other major global economies, should take the lead here. Some folks oppose this as compromising national sovereignty, but there are ways of solving that issue. One way to create such a system would be to reform and reorganize the International Monetary Fund (IMF), created in the wake of World War II. But it might be better and more acceptable globally to start from scratch, perhaps making the IMF part of the Global Reserve System.

Additionally, a number of financial regulatory reforms are needed in the U.S. itself. One of these is oversight of and limitations to millisecond program trading that week by week skims off millions of dollars from the stock market, enriching hedge funds and other financial firms but depressing economic growth and restricting wider distribution of wealth among the large body of small investors.

The United States could learn from Canada, which for decades has had a much more effective system of financial and banking regulations and thus escaped the worst effects of the recent financial crisis.

Benefits: It is untrue that the reforms mentioned here would cripple economic growth or limit prosperity. Quite the opposite! They would make the global financial system much more transparent, stable, and predictable, thus fostering economic health. This is the lesson of the U.S. Federal Reserve System and of the key financial reforms enacted at the time of the Great Depression (later partially dismantled by Congress in the 1990s and early twenty-first century).

Danger: If international finance is not reformed, the global economy will gyrate wildly due to currency and credit speculation. It will be like a weather system totally out of control. Poorer countries especially will be harmed, and the gap between rich and poor both nationally and globally will widen dramatically. The 1% will become ever richer and more politically powerful; the 99% will be the major victims.

A Catch-List of Other Reforms

The list of urgent reforms is nearly endless. Beyond the seven areas discussed above, other specific reforms would add to a larger reform momentum, to the benefit of all. Some examples:

Prison reform is urgent. As hinted above—and like so many issues—the problem here involves both causes and effects.

The percentage of citizens, especially African Americans, imprisoned in the U.S. is a national disgrace and a global scandal. Major reforms are needed in the legal and court system, especially, and also in the whole system of incarceration, which in recent decades has become more and more a for-profit business.

I have not listed this is one of the seven top priorities because several of the reforms I discuss, particularly in education and agriculture and food, would ameliorate the horrendous prison situation. However major reforms definitely are needed in this area, as well.

Postal Service reform. The government should undertake a major reform, probably through a public-private venture, to put the Postal Service on a sound financial footing. This will require some continuing government subsidy (as in most nations), since the Postal Service is a necessary public utility and shouldn't be expected fully to pay for itself.

One idea that should be considered is having United Parcel Service (UPS) take over responsibility for the United States Postal Service (USPS—just one letter difference!). An agreement could be reached that guarantees the continuation of all existing essential postal services (including six-day-a-week delivery and maintaining Post Offices in remote areas) while securing UPS against financial loss in the postal operation. Part of this should be the elimination of most "junk mail" (advertising flyers, catalogs, etc.), moving all such communication to the Internet and other channels. The result would be better postal service, more efficient management, and less drain on the federal budget.

The U.S. Congress. Two major reforms, especially, are urgent: A law prohibiting congressmen and women from serving as lobbyists for at least ten years after their terms end, and a prohibition on engaging in insider stock trading—that is, buying or selling stock based on confidential information they receive as part of the legislative process. Most congressmen leave Washington much richer than when they entered. The whole process tends to corrupt the people's business and needs reform, especially in these areas.

Other issues could be mentioned, and much more could be said about every issue discussed. No doubt readers will want to add other reforms they consider urgent. Viewed ecologically, however, these reforms would make a huge difference and would prompt positive action in other areas.

Conclusion

This is today's *New Reform Agenda*. But I quickly add three important caveats.

First, I have focused mainly on the United States because this is my current and primary context and because of the great influence the U.S. has globally. Much that is said here applies to other nations however, with proper adjustment and contextualization. And all needed reforms are in some sense global, given our ecological interdependence.

Second, these reforms are practical, not political in any partisan or ideological sense. They are pragmatic and "populist" in the best sense, benefiting everyone.

Third, most of this analysis focuses on economic, political, social, and environmental realities. But that is not the whole story.

I write as a committed Christian. I see the above analysis as an exercise in Christian love. But the most basic issues in our world are spiritual, and the most basic need is deep spiritual renewal—a great awakening—prompted by the Spirit of God.

Thus the resources of the church—prayer, worship, evangelism, servanthood, family life, and neighborhood-building—are urgently needed concerning all that is said here.

The greatest global need is revival, a Great Awakening, and the Triune God is the only and ultimate source of that.

We pray for that. Meanwhile we should join forces with all who seek the kinds of reforms that point in the direction of the ultimate kingdom of God.

From the standpoint of the being and mission of the church, the Christian discipleship answer to the issues discussed here are presented in my book with Joel Scandrett, *Salvation Means Creation Healed*.

December 9, 2011

# # #

www.ingramcontent.com/pod-product-compliance
Lightning Source LLC
Chambersburg PA
CBHW030014040426
42337CB00012BA/775